2 Peter & Jude

God's Plan for Spiritual Growth

JOHN A. STEWART

Lamplighters International is a Christian ministry that helps individuals engage with God and His Word and equips believers to be disciple-makers.

For additional information about Lamplighters ministry resources, contact:

Lamplighters International
771 NE Harding Street, Suite 250
Minneapolis, MN USA 55413
or visit our website at
www.LamplightersUSA.org.

Product Code 2PJ-NK-2P

ISBN 978-1-931372-74-9

CONTENTS

How to Use This Study

What Is Lamplighters?

Lamplighters is a Christian ministry that helps individuals engage with God and His Word and equips believers to be disciple-makers. This Bible study, comprising six individual lessons, is a self-contained unit and an integral part of the entire discipleship ministry. When you have completed the study, you will have a much greater understanding of a portion of God's Word, with many new truths that you can apply to your life.

How to study a Lamplighters Lesson

A Lamplighters study begins with prayer, your Bible, the weekly lesson, and a sincere desire to learn more about God's Word. The questions are presented in a progressive sequence as you work through the study material. You should not use Bible commentaries or other reference books (except a dictionary) until you have completed your weekly lesson and met with your weekly group. Approaching the Bible study in this way allows you to personally encounter many valuable spiritual truths from the Word of God.

To gain the most out of the Bible study, find a quiet place to complete your weekly lesson. Each lesson will take approximately 45–60 minutes to complete. You will likely spend more time on the first few lessons until you are familiar with the format, and our prayer is that each week will bring the discovery of important life principles.

The writing space within the weekly studies provides the opportunity for you to answer questions and respond to what you have learned. Putting answers in your own words, and including Scripture references where appropriate, will help you personalize and commit to memory the truths you have learned. The answers to the questions will be found in the Scripture references at the end of each question or in the passages listed at the beginning of each lesson.

If you are part of a small group, it's a good idea to record the specific dates that you'll be meeting to do the individual lessons. Record the specific dates each time the group will be meeting next to the lesson titles on the Contents page. Additional lines have been provided for you to record when you go through this same study at a later date.

The side margins in the lessons can be used for the spiritual insights you glean from other group or class members. Recording these spiritual truths will likely be a spiritual help to you and others when you go through this study again in the future.

AUDIO INTRODUCTION

A brief audio introduction is available to help you learn about the historical background of the book, gain an understanding of its theme and structure, and be introduced to some of the major truths. Audio introductions are available for all Lamplighters studies and are a great resource for the group leader; they can also be used to introduce the study to your group. To access the audio introductions, go to www.LamplightersUSA.org.

"DO YOU THINK?" QUESTIONS

Each weekly study has a few *"do you think?"* questions designed to help you to make personal applications from the biblical truths you are learning. In the first lesson the *"do you think?"* questions are placed in italic print for easy identification. If you are part of a study group, your insightful answers to these questions could be a great source of spiritual encouragement to others.

PERSONAL QUESTIONS

Occasionally you'll be asked to respond to personal questions. If you are part of a study group you may choose not to share your answers to these questions with the others. However, be sure to answer them for your own benefit because they will help you compare your present level of spiritual maturity to the biblical principles presented in the lesson.

A FINAL WORD

Throughout this study the masculine pronouns are frequently used in the generic sense to avoid awkward sentence construction. When the pronouns *he*, *him*, and *his* are used in reference to the Trinity (God the Father, Jesus Christ, and the Holy Spirit), they always refer to the masculine gender.

This Lamplighters study was written after many hours of careful preparation. It is our prayer that it will help you "... grow in the grace and knowledge of our Lord and Savior Jesus Christ. To Him be the glory both now and forever. Amen" (2 Peter 3:18).

What Is an Intentional Discipleship Bible Study?
The *Next Step* in Bible Study

The Lamplighters Bible study series is ideal for individual, small group, and classroom use. This Bible study is also designed for Intentional Discipleship training. An Intentional Discipleship (ID) Bible study has four key components. Individually they are not unique, but together they form the powerful core of the ID Bible study process.

1. Objective: Lamplighters is a discipleship training ministry that has a dual objective: (1) to help individuals engage with God and His Word and (2) to equip believers to be disciple-makers. The small group format provides extensive opportunity for ministry training, and it's not limited by facilities, finances, or a lack of leadership staffing.

2. Content: The Bible is the focus rather than Christian books. Answers to the study questions are included within the study guides, so the theology is in the study material, not in the leader's mind. This accomplishes two key objectives: (1) It gives the group leader confidence to lead another individual or small group without fear, and (2) it protects the small group from theological error.

3. Process: The ID Bible study process begins with an Open House, which is followed by a 6–14-week study, which is followed by a presentation of the Final Exam (see graphic on page 8). This process provides a natural environment for continuous spiritual growth and leadership development.

4. Leadership Development: As group participants grow in Christ, they naturally invite others to the groups. The leader-trainer (1) identifies and recruits new potential leaders from within the group, (2) helps them register for online discipleship training, and (3) provides in-class leadership mentoring until they are both competent and confident to lead a group according to the ID Bible study process. This leadership development process is scalable, progressive, and comprehensive.

OVERVIEW OF THE LEADERSHIP TRAINING AND DEVELOPMENT PROCESS

There are three stages of leadership training in the Intentional Discipleship process: (1) leading studies, (2) training leaders, and (3) multiplying groups (see appendix for greater detail).

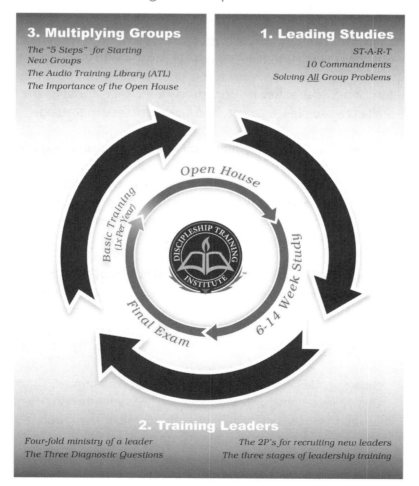

Intentional Discipleship
Training & Development Process

3. Multiplying Groups

The "5 Steps" for Starting New Groups
The Audio Training Library (ATL)
The Importance of the Open House

1. Leading Studies

ST-A-R-T
10 Commandments
Solving All Group Problems

Open House

Basic Training (1x Per Year)

6-14 Week Study

Final Exam

DISCIPLESHIP TRAINING INSTITUTE

2. Training Leaders

Four-fold ministry of a leader
The Three Diagnostic Questions

The 2P's for recruiting new leaders
The three stages of leadership training

How Can I Be Trained?

Included within this Bible study is the student workbook for Level 1 (Basic Training). Level 1 training is both free and optional. Level 1 training teaches you a simple 4-step process (ST-A-R-T) to help you prepare a life-changing Bible study and 10 proven small group leadership principles that will help your group thrive. To register for a Level 1 online training event, either as an individual or as a small group, go to www.LamplightersUSA.org/training or www.discipleUSA. org. If you have additional questions, you can also call 800-507-9516.

ONE

PRINCIPLES OF
SPIRITUAL GROWTH

Read 2 Peter 1:1–11;
other references as given.

God used Peter, apostle and fisherman, to write the letters known as 1 and 2 Peter. Religious liberals and critics have doubted Simon Peter's authorship of 2 Peter, questioning whether a simple fisherman could have written the book with its polished Greek language. Peter's bold declaration in 2 Peter 2:1 and his biographical account of the transfiguration (2 Peter 1:16–18) are two undeniable facts that refute their unwarranted claim.

It has been said that critics don't like 2 Peter for three reasons: chapter 1, chapter 2, and chapter 3. Chapter 1 presents a strong case for the doctrine of biblical inerrancy; chapter 2 exposes the theological errors of false teachers; and chapter 3 presents the sobering certainty of Christ's return—all distasteful doctrines to religious nonbelievers.

The apostle Peter revealed his purpose for writing this letter when he stated, **For this reason I will not be negligent to remind you always of these things, though you know and are established in the present truth. Yes, I think it is right, as long as I am in this tent, to stir you up by reminding you** (2 Peter 1:12–13). Second Peter is God's spiritual stimulus plan, and Peter wrote the letter to stir his readers, including you, to greater spiritual devotion.

Before you begin each lesson, ask God to reveal Himself through His Word and to transform you into the image of His Son.

Lombardi Time Rule:

If the leader arrives early, he or she has time to pray, prepare the room, and greet others personally.

———

ADD GROUP INSIGHTS BELOW

1. It has been said that when the apostle Paul put down his pen, the apostle Peter picked it up. Peter refers to Paul's writings and describes them as numerous and compatible with his own writings, but also difficult to understand by those who aren't knowledgeable in the Word and those who are spiritually weak (2 Peter 3:15).

   a. How does Peter introduce himself to his readers (2 Peter 1:1)?

   _____

   _____

   _____

   _____

   b. List four things that Peter says about the faith of his original readers (2 Peter 1:1–2).

   1. _____

   _____

   2. _____

   _____

   3. _____

   _____

   4. _____

   _____

2. Peter introduces himself as a **bondservant** (Greek *doulos*—slave, servant; NIV: "servant") and an **apostle** (Gk. *apostolos*—someone commissioned by another). He also says (all) believers have received a **like precious faith** (Gk. *isotimos*—the same honor, equal privilege, similar standing). If any verse in the Bible substantiates the old Christian cliché, "The ground is level at the foot of the cross," this is it!

   a. Many believers are confused about their true relationship to Jesus Christ. They think God provides eternal life, but they retain the right to run their lives and pursue their own dreams. What did Paul teach the Roman and Corinthian believers about their relationship to Christ that contradicts this erroneous perspective (Romans 6:19; 1 Corinthians 6:19)?

_____

_____

_____

_____

b. Jesus Christ called Peter to be an apostle—someone commissioned by a higher authority. What similar, yet distinct, commission has Jesus given every believer (Acts 1:8; 2 Corinthians 5:18–20)?

_____

_____

_____

3. When an individual is saved (born again), he is given God's saving grace and receives the gift of eternal life. At salvation, believers are given access by faith into an entirely new life (Romans 5:2). They also are recipients of God's sanctifying grace (divine power for living righteously) and peace, but they must learn how to live by faith if they expect to receive it.

a. The Bible says God has given us **all things that *pertain* to life and godliness** (2 Peter 1:3, emphasis added). What *do you think* this important phrase means?

_____

_____

_____

_____

Zip-It Rule:

Group members should agree to disagree, but should never be disagreeable.

ADDITIONAL INSIGHTS

b. The Bible repeats a key phrase that reveals how a believer receives God's grace and peace and everything else that pertains to life and godliness (2 Peter 1:2–3). What is this important phrase?

_____

_____

4. The first principle of spiritual growth is to understand that salvation is a gift (**have obtained like precious faith**; 2 Peter 1:1). Next, the believer must realize that God has given every believer the same kind of faith, and this faith is a precious gift from God—not something to be treated lightly or regarded of little value. God's spiritual growth plan continues when believers fully embrace their new identity (as Christ's servants) and accept their commission to be ambassadors for Christ (2 Peter 1:1). Then believers must realize that Christ has given them everything that pertains to life and godliness and **exceedingly great and precious promises** (2 Peter 1:4). What are some of these promises God makes available to all believers (Romans 15:13; 1 Corinthians 10:13; Philippians 4:7; 2 Timothy 1:7)?

_____

_____

_____

_____

_____

_____

5. Believers are given a *new nature* at the time of salvation (2 Corinthians 5:17), but they can become partakers of a *divine nature* if they respond to God's progressive sanctification process (2 Peter 1:4). Even though God commands believers to be diligent about their spiritual growth (2 Peter 1:5–11), many believers live spiritually anemic Christian lives. The late Dr. Henry Brandt said, "God gives every Christian the

right to live a miserable Christian life. It is not His will, but He will give you that much grace."

a. Every Christian should be diligent about his spiritual growth. What *do you think* are some evidences that a believer is serious about his or her personal spiritual development?

_____

_____

_____

_____

_____

b. Many Christians confuse their priorities in life. They worship their work, work at their play, and play at their worship. Are you diligent to be all God wants you to be, or are you leading an apathetic Christian life—one characterized by anxiety, fear, worry, doubts, anger, unforgiveness, an inability to overcome sinful habits, confusion about your relationship to Christ and other evidences of spiritual immaturity?

_____

_____

_____

6. Peter presents eight spiritual qualities that all believers should incorporate into their spiritual lives (2 Peter 1:5–7). It is interesting that **virtue** (Gk. *arete*—virtue, moral excellence; NIV: "goodness") is listed before knowledge. While (right) knowing always precedes (right) doing or actions (John 8:32), it can also be true that, as the ancient philosopher Plato said, "a man's morality dictates his theology." Some Christians never really mature spiritually because they aren't willing to give up vices (sin) in their lives.

Want to learn how to disciple another person, lead a life-changing Bible study or start another study? Go to www.Lamplighters USA.org/training to learn how.

ADDITIONAL INSIGHTS

a. What promises are given to those who actively allow God to incorporate these eight qualities into their lives (2 Peter 1:8, 10–11)?

_____

_____

_____

b. A Christian forfeits grace, peace, and God's exceedingly great and precious promises when he is unwilling to grow spiritually. Name at least four negative results a Christian will experience if he or she is *not* diligent about spiritual growth (2 Peter 1:9; 1 Corinthians 3:11–15; 1 John 2:28).

_____

_____

_____

_____

_____

_____

c. If you are a Christian, how did God use this portion of His Word to challenge you to be more diligent in your Christian life?

_____

_____

_____

_____

_____

Two

God's Inerrant Word

Read 2 Peter 1:12–21;
other references as given.

In the first lesson (2 Peter 1:1–11), Peter told his readers that they had received the same kind of faith as God had given the apostles. He also said they could become partakers of the divine nature and direct beneficiaries of God's exceedingly great and precious promises—but on one condition: they must be diligent about their spiritual growth. If they were complacent, God's only promises to them were spiritual unfruitfulness and shortsightedness—even to the point of doubting their eternal relationship to Jesus Christ.

In 2 Peter 1:12–21, Peter explains why he wrote the letter (2 Peter 1:12–15), recounts the ultimate spiritual experience (2 Peter 1:16–18) and concludes the first chapter with one of the clearest statements on the doctrine of inerrancy in the entire Bible (2 Peter 1:19–21).

Now ask God to reveal Himself through His Word and to transform you into the image of His Son.

1. The words **For this reason I will not be negligent to remind you** (2 Peter 1:12; NIV: "So I will always remind you") can point back to the previous verses or forward to a reason about to be stated. Do you think the phrase **for this reason** refers to (1) the previous passage about spiritual growth (2 Peter 1:2–11) or (2) the verses just after verse 12, or (3) is it the general theme of his letter (2 Peter 1:12, 15; 3:1)? Why?

Volunteer Rule:

If the leader asks for volunteers to read, pray, and answer the questions, group members will be more inclined to invite newcomers.

ADD GROUP
INSIGHTS BELOW

17

_____

_____

_____

2. a. Peter exhorted his readers (including us) to pursue spiritual diligence (vs. 12–15). What words and phrases indicate Peter's urgent desire for the spiritual advancement of his readers (2 Peter 1:12–15)?

_____

_____

_____

_____

_____

b. The apostle Paul also wanted his readers to become mature in Christ. How did Paul describe his concern for the spiritual advancement of the Galatian Christians (Galatians 4:19)?

_____

_____

_____

_____

c. On a scale of 1 (not concerned at all) to 10 (passionately concerned, praying earnestly, living a godly life, reaching the lost, and encouraging believers), how concerned are you about the spiritual advancement of others, including their salvation, including those in your immediate family?

_____

3. A Christian cannot become spiritually mature without gaining the knowledge of God, and the knowledge of God cannot be acquired without knowing the Word of God. The late professor Howard Hendricks offered this excellent definition

of spiritual maturity: *"Bible + Obedience + Time = Spiritual Maturity."*

a. Peter's spiritual diligence was also demonstrated by his unwillingness to preach cleverly devised fables (Gk. *muthos*—myths, fables). "Fables" refers to mythical stories about gods, as well as mere speculations about the creation of the world and miraculous happenings (2 Peter 1:16). Rather than teaching unprovable myths, what did Peter emphasize in his teaching (2 Peter 1:16)?

_____

_____

_____

b. What are some things "careless" religious leaders teach rather than faithfully proclaiming God's Word (Mark 7:8–13; Colossians 2:8; 1 Timothy 1:3–4, 7–9; 2 Timothy 4:3–4)?

_____

_____

_____

_____

4. Jesus invited the apostles Peter, James, and John to witness the ultimate spiritual experience. The three apostles saw Moses and Elijah talking with Jesus as He was transfigured before them (Matthew 17:1–8). Yet in Peter's recounting of this miraculous event, he emphasized what God *said* rather than what he himself *saw*. Moreover, Peter didn't emphasize that others should listen to him just because he witnessed this amazing event. What was Peter's main point in recounting this miraculous event (2 Peter 1:19)?

_____

_____

59:59 Rule:

Participants appreciate when the leader starts and finishes the studies on time—all in one hour (the 59:59 rule). If the leader doesn't complete the entire lesson, the participants will be less likely to do their weekly lessons and the Bible study discussion will tend to wander.

———

ADDITIONAL INSIGHTS

5. a. What admonition did Peter give his readers (and all believers) regarding their response to the prophetic Word of God (2 Peter 1:19)?

    _____

    _____

    b. Peter told his readers they would **do well to heed** (NIV: "pay attention to") the prophetic Word (2 Peter 1:19) **until the day dawns and the morning star rises in your hearts.** What do you think this means, and when will it occur?

    _____

    _____

    _____

    c. What warning did the writer of Hebrews give his readers if they failed to heed God's Word (Hebrews 2:1–3)?

    _____

    _____

    _____

6. The phrase **no prophecy of Scripture is of any private interpretation** (2 Peter 1:20) has been variously understood: (1) Scripture should be interpreted only in context, meaning individual prophecies must be interpreted in light of other prophecies; (2) Scriptures shouldn't be interpreted according to one's own desire; (3) Scripture cannot be interpreted without the aid of the Holy Spirit; and (4) Old Testament prophecies did not originate in the minds of the prophets themselves. Which one of these interpretations do you think is the correct interpretation (2 Peter 1:20–22)?

    _____

    _____

    _____

35% Rule:

If the leader talks
more than 35% of
the time, the group
members will be
less likely
to participate.

ADDITIONAL
INSIGHTS

_____

_____

7. There are a myriad of views related to the doctrine of biblical inspiration: (1) Some people believe the Bible is a non-inspired, archaic collection of lies, fabrications, and distortions—a crutch for the weak and an impediment to social advancement; (2) others believe the Bible is a collection of God's inspired words and man's best thoughts—a spiritual compilation that must be the work of early editors (redactors); and (3) others believe that Scripture is the divinely inspired, inerrant Word of God.

   a. Which view of biblical inspiration does the Bible teach is correct?

   _____

   b. What does the Bible say about its origin and accuracy (2 Timothy 3:16; 2 Peter 1:20–21)?

   _____

   _____

   c. Jesus told the Pharisees that **the Scripture cannot be broken** (John 10:35). What do you think this means and how does this verse apply to the theory that the Scriptures are a collection of God's Word and man's thoughts (see #2 above)?

   _____

   _____

   _____

   _____

8. The Bible unequivocally claims divine inspiration. The historical accuracy of the Bible, the fulfillment of many Old Testament prophecies, and the discovery of many

archeological finds authenticate its claim as the inerrant, infallible Word of God. What does the Bible also teach about its sufficiency (2 Timothy 3:16–17)?

_____

_____

_____

_____

Three

False Teachers

Read 2 Peter 2:1–22;
other references as given.

In 2 Peter 1, the apostle encouraged his readers to grow spiritually. Faith in God's Word—not myths, fables, genealogies, man-made religious traditions, or secular psychology—is the means by which a Christian's faith is advanced. Even powerful religious experiences, such as the one Peter had when Moses, Elijah, and Jesus were transfigured before him, must be evaluated from the spiritual perspective of what God's Word says, not from the perspective of the experience itself.

In 2 Peter 2, the apostle reveals the reason for his passionate appeal for his readers' spiritual growth. False teachers, like the false prophets who plagued ancient Israel, will invade the church and lead many astray. Only those who are armed with God's Word and who are growing spiritually will escape their deceptive attacks. Peter's description of these spiritual parasites' motives and methods is as instructive today as it was 2,000 years ago.

Now ask God to reveal Himself through His Word and to transform you into the image of His Son.

1. During Old Testament times and early New Testament times, God called men and women to deliver His messages of instruction, warning, and coming judgment to individuals and nations. God's prophets received (1) a supernatural ability to receive messages directly from God and (2) God's authority to deliver His messages accurately to a prescribed audience. Interestingly, the Bible teaches that God did

Focus Rule:

If the leader helps the group members focus on the Bible, they will gain confidence to study God's Word on their own.

ADD GROUP
INSIGHTS BELOW

23

nothing without first revealing it to His prophets (Amos 3:7).

a. God also allowed false prophets to exist and even speak to His people (2 Peter 2:1). False prophets, claiming to be God's messengers, deceived many and brought great harm to the nation of Israel. Why did God allow these false prophets to exist (Deuteronomy 13:1–4)?

_____

_____

b. How could the Israelites determine if a prophet was a true messenger of God or a false prophet (Deuteronomy 18:20–22)?

_____

_____

_____

_____

c. Making a false claim to be one of God's prophets was a very serious matter. What was the penalty for those who claimed to speak for God but were not His true prophets (Deuteronomy 18:20)?

_____

_____

2. God's true prophets were to be careful to say and do all He commanded (Joshua 1:8). First Kings 13 records a tragic story of an unnamed prophet whose spiritual carelessness cost him his life (1 Kings 13:1–24).

a. How could the unnamed prophet (man of God) have known that the older prophet (also unnamed) was lying and not speaking from God's authority (1 Kings 13:14–22; see also verses 8–11)?

_____

_____

_____

_____

b. How do you think Christians can apply this important
    principle to their lives?

    _____

    _____

    _____

    _____

3. Both Jesus and Paul warned others about false prophets
    and teachers. How did they describe these enemies of God
    (Matthew 7:15; Acts 20:29–30)?

    _____

    _____

4. a. Look closely at the apostle Peter's description of the
        false teachers in 2 Peter 2. Do you think these false
        teachers were Christians who erroneously believe false
        doctrine and were teaching it to others (2 Peter 2:1, 14,
        20–21), or were they religious infidels (unbelievers) who
        were posing as genuine believers (2 Peter 2:1, 3, 9, 12–
        13, 17, 22)? Why?

        _____

        _____

        _____

        _____

    b. If these false teachers were not saved, what do you
        think is the meaning of the phrase **even denying the
        Lord who bought them** (2 Peter 2:1)?

        _____

Drawing Rule:

To learn how to
draw everyone
into the group
discussion without
calling on anyone,
go to
www.Lamplighters
USA.org/training.

_____

ADDITIONAL
INSIGHTS

25

_____

_____

_____

5. The apostle Peter said false teachers **secretly bring in destructive heresies** (2 Peter 2:1). What do you think are some ways false teachers secretly introduce destructive heresies (2 Peter 2:1; Genesis 3:1; 2 Timothy 4:3–4)?

_____

_____

_____

_____

_____

6. a. List several words and phrases that describe the *motives* of false teachers (2 Peter 2:1, 3, 10, 14–15).

_____

_____

_____

b. Who is their primary target audience (2 Peter 2:14, 18)?

_____

_____

_____

c. List several words and phrases that describe the *methods* of false teachers (2 Peter 2:1, 3, 12, 14, 18–19).

_____

_____

_____

_____

d. How effective are they (2 Peter 2:2)?

_____

_____

Is your study going well? Consider starting a new group. To learn how, go to www. Lamplighters USA.org/training.

ADDITIONAL INSIGHTS

7. In 2 Peter 2:4–10, the apostle presents three illustrations of God's righteous judgment. The first illustration (v. 4, the angels who sinned) appears to refer to the ancient rebellion of Lucifer and a third of the angelic world (Isaiah 14:12–15) or to angels who cohabited with women (Genesis 6:1–4). The second illustration (v. 5) refers to the worldwide flood and God's deliverance of Noah and his family (Genesis 6:5). The third illustration (vs. 6–8) refers to the destruction of Sodom and Gomorrah and God's deliverance of Abraham's nephew Lot during the overthrow of the cities (Genesis 19:1–29).

a. List at least three spiritual truths the Bible teaches about God's judgment (2 Peter 2:4–10).

1. _____

    _____ (v. _____)

2. _____

    _____ (v. _____)

3. _____

    _____ (v. _____)

b. How could you apply the spiritual truths you listed in #7a to your life?

_____

_____

8. a. Peter said the false teachers had **eyes full of adultery** (2 Peter 2:14). What do you think this means?

_____

_____

_____

_____

b. The Bible uses the word *adultery* to refer to marital
    unfaithfulness (Matthew 5:32) and spiritual unfaithfulness
    (James 4:4). If you're single, do you consider the
    opposite sex to be God's creation, or are your eyes filled
    with (sexual) adultery toward them? If you are married,
    are you satisfied with your spouse, or are your eyes filled
    with adultery toward other people? If you have lust over
    other people, what do you think you could do to honor
    God more in this area of your life?

_____

_____

_____

FOUR

THE DAY OF THE LORD

**Read 2 Peter 3:1–18;
other references as given.**

The apostle Peter exhorted his readers to be *diligent* about their spiritual growth (2 Peter 1). Next, the apostle exhorted his readers to be *discerning* about the religious teachers they allowed to influence their spiritual lives (2 Peter 2).

In 2 Peter 3 Peter exhorts his readers to be *determined* to live with a sense of daily anticipation of Christ's return. Scoffers, writes Peter, will question the authority of God's Word by openly casting doubt on the reality of Christ's return.

Now ask God to reveal Himself through His Word and to transform you into the image of His Son.

1. What was Peter's primary motivation for writing the letter known as 2 Peter (2 Peter 3:1–2)?

   _____

   _____

2. a. Give three specific reasons why Christians need to be reminded of spiritual truth (Luke 8:5–13). Support your answers with specific verse references.

   1. _____

      _____ (v. _____)

   2. _____

      _____ (v. _____)

Gospel Gold
Rule:

Try to get all the answers to the questions—not just the easy ones. Go for the gold.

———

ADD GROUP
INSIGHTS BELOW

3. _____

    _____ (v. _____)

b. Of the three reasons why believers need to be reminded of spiritual truth in Luke 8:5–13, which one do you think is the biggest threat to your spiritual advancement? Why?

    _____

    _____

    _____

c. What specific steps do you need to take to overcome this spiritual deterrent?

    _____

    _____

    _____

3. Many Christians ignore the Old Testament, believing it offers only limited spiritual help for the Christian. But our minds are stirred up to greater spiritual devotion to God when we study both the Old Testament (**the holy prophets**; v. 2) and the New Testament.

    List three additional benefits of studying the Old Testament (Romans 15:4; 1 Corinthians 10:11; 2 Timothy 3:14–17).

    _____

    _____

    _____

    _____

    _____

    _____

4. The apostle Peter has dealt with two of the believer's greatest spiritual threats to his spiritual advancement:

(personal) apathy and (theological) apostasy. Beginning in 2 Peter 3:3, Peter deals with another enemy of the believer's growth: a spiritual complacency resulting from uncertainty about Christ's return.

a. What was the main argument of the scoffers who doubted Jesus Christ's physical return to earth (2 Peter 3:4)?

_____

_____

_____

b. What do you think is meant by the statement **this they willfully forget** (v. 5; NIV: "deliberately forget")? What is another way of saying the same thing?

_____

_____

_____

c. What argument does Peter use to refute their erroneous perspective (2 Peter 3:5–7)?

_____

_____

_____

_____

5. The phrase **with the Lord one day is as a thousand years** (2 Peter 3:8) is often used as scriptural support by those who believe in the "day–age" theory of creation. Proponents of this theological interpretation believe the word **day** (Hebrew: *yom*; Genesis 1), refers to an age or extended period of time rather than a literal 24-hour day.

a. Why shouldn't this specific phrase in 2 Peter 3:8 be

Balance Rule:

To learn how to balance the group discussion, go to www.Lamplighters USA.org/training.

———

ADDITIONAL INSIGHTS

used as scriptural support for the "day–age" theory of creation?

_____

_____

b. What is the point of Peter's argument in 2 Peter 3:8?

_____

_____

c. Why has Christ waited so long to return to earth (2 Peter 3:9, 14–15)?

_____

_____

_____

6. The **day of the Lord** (2 Peter 3:10) describes end-time events that begin with the unannounced return ("like a thief"; v. 10 NIV) of Jesus Christ to earth at the beginning of the tribulation period and culminates with the beginning of eternity.

a. The Lord destroyed the world with a universal flood (Genesis 7:1–9:17) because of wickedness (Genesis 6:3–7). Why will God destroy the world again, and what will be the manner and extent of its destruction (2 Peter 3:7, 10, 12)?

_____

_____

_____

b. Peter asks a rhetorical question in 2 Peter 3:11 and then answers it for his readers. Since believers know this world is going to be destroyed and God will judge the ungodly, what should Christians be doing (Colossians

1:28; 2 Peter 3:11–12, 14)?

_____

_____

It's time to choose your next study. Turn to the back of the study guide for a list of available studies or go online for the latest studies.

ADDITIONAL
INSIGHTS

7. The **new heavens and a new earth** are first mentioned in 2 Peter 3:13, but they are described in more detail in Revelation 21:1–22:5. What are some notable characteristics of the new heaven and the new earth (2 Peter 3:13; Revelation 21:1–4, 10–17, 22–24)?

_____

_____

_____

_____

8. Christ's return to earth is not delayed because of defeat, disinterest or dereliction of duty. God's mercy—demonstrated in His unfathomable patience toward unrepentant sinners—stays His wrath and withholds His hand of righteous judgment (2 Peter 3:15). Even the willful ignorance of the scoffers, driven by their own lusts (2 Peter 3:3), does not provoke God to act perniciously (highly injurious or destructive, deadly) or contrary to His sovereign will.

    a. What final warning does Peter give all believers (v. 17, beloved; NIV: "dear friends")?

    _____

    _____

    b. What are two things every Christian is admonished to do to become spiritually mature (2 Peter 3:18)?

        1. _____

        2. _____

ADDITIONAL INSIGHTS

FIVE

CONTEND FOR THE FAITH

Read Jude 1–10; other references as given.

Gnosticism (from the Greek noun *gnosis*: knowledge, pronounced *NOSS-te-siz-em*) was a heresy that began to develop late in the first century AD that became a significant problem in the second-century Christian church. Central to its teaching were the following concepts: (1) matter was evil and spirit was good, (2) knowledge was superior to virtue, (3) Scripture was to be interpreted non-literally and could be understood only by a select few, (4) evil in the world precluded (ruled out in advance) God being the only Creator, (5) Jesus Christ did not come in the flesh, and (6) there would be no resurrection of the body.

This heresy led its more ardent followers to exhibit the dual characteristics of moral bankruptcy and spiritual arrogance—a strange combination of vices that plagues some Christian leaders today. If all matter is evil, the Gnostics said, and there is no way to change it, then eat, drink, and be immoral. Although not all Gnostics were licentious (some were ascetics), they believed that salvation was gained by acquiring a superior inner knowledge of God, which was available to a select few.

Jude's letter, originally intended to articulate the truths of salvation (Jude 3), was redirected by the Holy Spirit to confront this emerging heresy. Jude's letter continues to be a clarion call to all believers to earnestly contend for the faith that was once for all entrusted to the saints.

Now ask God to reveal Himself through His Word and to transform you into the image of His Son.

Many groups study the Final Exam the week after the final lesson for three reasons: (1) someone might come to Christ, (2) believers gain assurance of salvation, (3) group members learn how to share the gospel.

———

ADD GROUP INSIGHTS BELOW

1. Jude (Hebrew *Judah*; Gk. *Ioudas* or *Joudas*) introduces himself as a bondservant of Jesus Christ and brother of James (Jude 1). Many Bible scholars believe he was the half-brother of Christ (Matthew 13:55). List three things Jude said in his initial description of his readers that are true of all believers (Jude 1).

_____

_____

_____

_____

_____

_____

2. In Peter's second letter, the apostle said believers had received a precious faith (2 Peter 1:1). Now Jude exhorts or beseeches his readers to **contend earnestly for the faith** (Jude 3). The Greek word (*epagonizesthai*) used for **contend** means to struggle for, to exercise great effort and exertion for something. The word was used of athletic contests and the struggle and efforts of athletes in their games.

   a. In Jude 3, the phrase **the faith** (*pistis*; verb *pisteo*) refers to God's completed revelation to man as revealed through the Holy Scriptures. List at least two ways or means through which error is often propagated or passed along to others in this world (false religions, including Christian sects that don't adhere to the Bible as the inerrant, infallible Word of God).

      1. _____

      2. _____

      3. _____

   b. List at least one thing you could do to fulfill the biblical command to earnestly **contend for the faith** and fight against evil for each of the areas you listed in question 2a.

_____

_____

Transformation Rule:

Seek for personal transformation, not mere information, from God's Word.

___

ADDITIONAL INSIGHTS

3. Believers are to defend God's Word, which was **once for all delivered to the saints** (Jude 3). What do you think this important phrase means, and how does this verse apply to those who claim to speak for God (Mohammed, Joseph Smith [Mormons], Charles Taze Russell [Jehovah's Witnesses], Mary Baker Eddy [Christian Science], and modern self-proclaimed prophets)?

_____

_____

_____

4. Biblical theology is the study of God as He has revealed Himself through His inspired Word. It is the means by which believers learn God's attributes and grow in their faith. It's been said that the believer who doesn't study God's Word has no advantage over the person who doesn't have a Bible.

   a. Name two key doctrines of the Christian faith that the spiritual imposters misunderstood, thus leading to their own destruction and the spiritual harm of others (Jude 4).

      1. _____

      2. _____

   b. The Bible says **certain men have crept in unnoticed** (Jude 4; NIV: "have secretly slipped in among you") into the churches. Why do you think true believers allow this to happen (Jude 4, 16)?

_____

_____

_____

_____

_____

c. What should every church do to prevent apostates (spiritual liberals/religious nonbelievers) from gaining positions of spiritual leadership and spreading their false doctrine (1 Timothy 3:1–12; 5:22; 2 Timothy 4:2–4)?

_____

_____

_____

5. Many Christians misinterpret the doctrine of grace, regarding it as God's license for their own worldly behavior. If a Christian abuses his freedom in Christ, his hypocritical behavior will hinder his witness for Christ and cause younger believers to stumble in their relationship with God (1 Corinthians 8:9).

a. What instruction did the apostle Paul give the Galatian churches regarding the doctrine of grace and its legitimate expression toward others (Galatians 5:13; NKJV: **liberty**; NIV: "freedom")?

_____

_____

b. List three things Paul taught about how a believer should exercise his God-given freedom in Christ (1 Corinthians 8:9, 13; 9:19–22).

1. _____

   _____ (v. _____)

2. _____

   _____ (v. _____)

3. _____

   _____ (v. _____)

6. Jude presents three examples of God's judgment: (1) unbelievers who followed Moses during the Exodus (Jude 5), (2) angels who rebelled against Him (Jude 6), and (3) Sodom and Gomorrah and the surrounding cities that were destroyed (Jude 7). God's point is clear: Both Christians and spiritual imposters shouldn't assume that His willingness to allow false teachers to exist among His people is His endorsement of their sin. God will eventually judge all who rebel against Him!

No-Trespassing Rule:

To keep the Bible study on track, avoid talking about political parties, church denominations, and Bible translations.

ADDITIONAL INSIGHTS

a. The nonbelievers who followed Moses during the Exodus faced God's judgment (Jude 5). The angels who abandoned **their proper domain** (NIV 1984: "their own home") were judged when God imprisoned them in darkness until the time He will execute their final judgment (v. 6). Why were the cities of Sodom and Gomorrah judged (Jude 7)?

_____

_____

_____

b. Jude wrote that Sodom, Gomorrah and the other cities **are set forth as an example** (Jude 7). In what way do you think they serve as an example for us today?

_____

_____

_____

7. The phrase **these dreamers** (Jude 8; NASB: "also by dreaming") indicates the spiritual imposters' "authority" likely came from their own prideful imagination rather than God's Word. Instead of having a healthy respect for the power of the demonic world (NASB: "angelic majesties"; NIV: "celestial beings"), they spoke arrogantly against things they knew very little about. Even the archangel Michael didn't do that. What do you think is a proper perspective

2 Peter & Jude: God's Plan for Spiritual Growth

for a Christian to have regarding the demonic powers of this world (Ephesians 6:10–18; 1 John 4:2–4)?

_____

_____

_____

_____

_____

8. God's judgment will come upon all nonbelievers, including those who masquerade as spiritual leaders within the church. How does he describe these spiritual imposters (Jude 8, 10)?

_____

_____

_____

_____

_____

Six

Faultless in His Presence

Read Jude 11–25;
other references as given.

Dreamers who **defile the flesh; ungodly men, who turn the grace of our God into lewdness; brute beasts.** These are the bold brush strokes that God uses to paint the ugly portrait of spiritual imposters who secretly infiltrate the church and cause great spiritual destruction. And like all who have masqueraded as genuine believers before them, they will ultimately face God's judgment.

In Jude 11–25, Jude pronounces God's ultimate expression of coming judgment (**Woe to them!**) on the spiritual imposters (Jude 11), gives a further description of their character and conduct (Jude 12–16), offers some positive spiritual counsel for his readers (Jude 17–23) and concludes his letter with one of the most beautiful doxologies in the Bible (Jude 24–25).

Now ask God to reveal Himself through His Word and to transform you into the image of His Son.

It's time to order your next study. Allow enough time to get the books so you can distribute them at the Open House. Consider ordering 2-3 extra books for newcomers.

ADD GROUP
INSIGHTS BELOW

1. The phrase **Woe to them!** is God's solemn pronouncement of coming judgment on all who pillage His church and scatter His sheep. A true shepherd *feeds* the sheep, but a hireling (one who serves for hire for purely selfish reasons) *feeds on* the sheep.

    a. List three more ways Jude describes the spiritual imposters (Jude 11).

    1. _____

2. _____

3. _____

    b. What do you think is meant by the phrase **they have gone in the way of Cain** (Jude 11; Genesis 4:1–7)?

_____

_____

_____

    c. What do you think is meant by the phrase **the error of Balaam** (Jude 11; Numbers 22:21–31; 31:16; 2 Peter 2:15–16)?

_____

_____

_____

2. Jude said the apostates had **perished** in the rebellion of Korah (Jude 11), but Korah was an Old Testament character who rejected Moses and led a revolt of 250 people against God's anointed leader (Numbers16:1–40). Why do you think the Bible pictured the spiritual imposters' judgment as having taken place in the past when it was clearly still future at the time of Jude's letter?

_____

_____

_____

3. The early church held corporate fellowship meals known as love feasts (Jude 12). Love feasts often included the Lord's Supper (communion) and were regarded as a sacred time of remembering Jesus' sacrifice on their behalf. It was also an opportunity for believers to express brotherly love and commitment to the Lord and each other. Apostates had invaded these sacred events and were exploiting the

Christians, serving themselves rather than Christ. List the four images Jude uses, all from the world of nature, to describe these spiritual imposters (Jude 12–13).

_____

_____

_____

_____

_____

_____

_____

_____

Final Exam:

Are you meeting next week to study the Final Exam? To learn how to present it effectively, contact Lamplighters.

———

ADDITIONAL INSIGHTS

4. The apostates were oblivious to God's coming judgment. Perhaps they thought that they were true believers because they worshipped with the genuine Christians in the church. Every Sunday three groups of people go to church: (1) believers (those who are truly saved or born again according to the Bible); (2) make-believers (non-Christians who participate in the regular gatherings of God's people and act somewhat like Christians); and (3) nonbelievers (those who are not Christians and don't pretend to be). Are you absolutely certain you are a true believer/Christian, or are you a make-believer? If you are uncertain what it means to be born again, please read the Final Exam at the end of this study guide. It will explain how you can become a true Christian.

_____

_____

_____

_____

_____

5. Enoch was an Old Testament prophet who prophesied about God's coming judgment on the spiritual imposters (Jude 14). The Lord Jesus Himself will judge them when He returns with His saints (Jude 15). How does the Bible describe the apostates, their actions and their motives in light of God's coming judgment (Jude 15)?

_____

_____

_____

6. List five additional characteristics of these spiritual impos-ters (Jude 16, 19).

_____

_____

_____

_____

7. Some Christians are dangerously naïve about spiritual attack within the church from false teachers, while others see themselves as "God cops" who must hunt down every theological error. The former are oblivious to the threat of theological error in others, and the latter are oblivious to theological error within themselves.

    a. What spiritual counsel did Jude give his readers to keep themselves from theological error and avoid being spiritually entrapped by the false teachers (Jude 17–18, 20–21)?

    _____

    _____

    _____

    _____

b. What do you think it means to **keep yourselves in the love of God** (Jude 21; NIV: "keep yourselves in God's love")?

_____

_____

_____

c. What responsibility do Christians have toward other believers who struggle with doubts and others who have fallen prey to false teaching (Jude 22–23)?

_____

_____

d. The phrase **hating even the garment defiled by the flesh** (Jude 23; NIV: "hating even the clothing stained by corrupted flesh") seems extreme. What important spiritual truth do you think this vivid word picture teaches?

_____

_____

_____

_____

8. The believer should be alert to spiritual danger and be confident that he can stand in faith with God's help (Jude 24). What else should the Christian be confident of (Jude 24)? Does that include you?

_____

_____

9. What does the Bible teach about God's character that should give every believer total confidence that He can fulfill every promise in His Word, including the one to present them faultless before Him with exceeding joy (Jude 25)?

Would you like to learn how to lead someone through this same study? It's not hard. Go to www.Lamplighters USA.org to register for *free* online leadership training.

———

ADDITIONAL INSIGHTS

_____

_____

_____

10. What did you learn from this study of 2 Peter and Jude about:

a.   God's plan for spiritual growth (2 Peter 1)?

_____

_____

_____

b.   False teachers and spiritual imposters (2 Peter 2; Jude)?

_____

_____

_____

c.   The return of Jesus Christ (2 Peter 3; Jude 14–15)?

_____

_____

_____

• • • •

Congratulations!

You have just finished a challenging study of 2 Peter and Jude. Hopefully you have a clearer understanding of the principles of spiritual growth and will be more alert to the spiritual dangers of false teachers. Hopefully you also have a better understanding of the day of the Lord. Most of all, it is our sincere hope that this study of 2 Peter and Jude has helped you grow in grace and in the knowledge of our Lord and Savior, Jesus Christ (2 Peter 3:18). Now contend for the faith which was once for all entrusted to the saints.

LEADER'S GUIDE

Lesson 1: Principles of Spiritual Growth

1. a. As a servant/bondservant and an apostle. Peter's use of the word *bondservant* indicates he understood the full extent of Christ's sacrifice on the cross on his behalf and willingly embraced his new position as His servant or slave. Peter's use of the word *apostle* indicates he willingly accepted Christ's commission to be His emissary or witness to spread the message of Christ's redemption to the world.
    b. 1. He said his readers had received the gift of faith. It was not something they earned by virtuous behavior.
        2. He said the gift of faith was precious.
        3. He said the gift of faith was the same as the apostles had received.
        4. He said the gift of faith was a result of the righteousness of Jesus Christ.

2. a. Romans 6:19: Prior to salvation, man is a slave to sin (uncleanness). After salvation, he is to present himself as a slave to righteousness. Prior to salvation, nonbelievers continually present themselves (their bodies) to uncleanness or sin, making them slaves of unrighteousness. After salvation, they are to present or offer themselves to God as slaves to righteousness for holiness. Paul's command indicates believers have the power (through the indwelling presence and ministry of the Holy Spirit) to choose to live righteously. He also said that they would be a slave either way: either to sin or to righteousness.
        1 Corinthians 6:19: Believers should realize (**do you not know?**) that their bodies are not their own because they have been bought with a price: the blood of Jesus Christ. Their bodies are the temple of the Holy Spirit who was given at salvation to every believer. All believers belong completely to God.
    b. Peter and the other apostles received a divine commission from Jesus Christ to be His witnesses, and believers have received a divine commission to be His ambassadors.

3. a. This is one of the most amazing promises in the Bible. The promise is

based upon God's divine power (Gk. *theios*—"divine"—is used only three times in Scripture), which guarantees its fulfillment. The Greek word for power (*dunamis*) is the same word from which the English word *dynamite* is derived. God's powerful promise to the believer contains two provisions: God's willingness to provide the believer with everything he needs for spiritual vitality (life) and for godly living. While other verses in God's Word speak to the inerrancy of Scripture (2 Timothy 3:16; 2 Peter 1:21), this verse speaks to the sufficiency of Scripture.

b. **In/through the knowledge of God/of Him who called us**, which means it is through acquiring the true knowledge of God that the believer can become a partaker of the divine nature.

4. 1. Believers can be filled with hope in this life through the power of the Holy Spirit (Romans 15:13).
   2. Believers can be assured God will give them grace to overcome all temptations (1 Corinthians 10:13).
   3. Believers can have control of their emotions and thoughts through Jesus Christ (Philippians 4:7).
   4. Believers can live free from fear and have their thoughts, emotions, and actions characterized by **love**, wisdom (**a sound mind**), and victorious living (**power**) (2 Timothy 1:7).

5. a. 1. The believer is engaged in personal and corporate worship, daily Bible reading, prayer and confession of sin.
   2. The believer exhibits a growing manifestation of the fruit of the Spirit (Galatians 5:22–23).
   3. The believer exhibits a growing desire to serve God and others.
   4. The believer exhibits a growing desire to reach the lost.
   5. Other answers could apply.

   b. Answers will vary.

6. a. 1. The believer will not be barren (v. 8; NIV: "ineffective"). 2. The believer will not be unfruitful (v. 8; Gk. *akarpos*—not fruitful), which means that he will manifest the fruit of the Spirit. 3. He will never stumble in relationship with God (v. 10). He will be richly welcomed into the presence and kingdom of God (v. 11).

   b. 1. The believer will become spiritually shortsighted or blind, meaning he will not begin to doubt his original, genuine conversion to Christ (v. 9). Notice that Peter doesn't say he will have lost his salvation but that the person will *forget* that he was purified from his former sins. 2. The believer will also suffer loss of eternal reward (1 Corinthians 3:11–15). 3. The believer can lose confidence to stand before God and not be ashamed when Christ returns (1 John 2:28). The shame is the result of the believer's failure to live wholeheartedly for the Lord, knowing that Christ had given His all for his salvation. The believer will also be ashamed that much of his earthly efforts were spent on things that were burned up (1 Corinthians 3:13–15).

c. Answers will vary.

Lesson 2: God's Inerrant Word

1. Initially, it appears Peter's admonishment to his readers is an appropriate personal application to his teaching in the previous section (vs. 2–11). Additional similar references in 2 Peter 1:15 and 3:1, however, offer strong evidence that 2 Peter 1:12 is Peter's first of three appeals to stir up his readers to greater spiritual devotion and the dominant theme of the letter. Peter, knowing that he would soon die, wanted to exhort believers to live unreservedly for God (2 Peter 1:14).

2. a. 1. I will not be negligent (v. 12). 2. Remind you always (v. 12). 3. As long as I am in this [earthly] tent (v. 13). 4. To stir you up (v. 13). 5. I think it is right (v. 13). 6. I will be careful (v. 15). 7. You always have a reminder (v. 15).

   b. Paul said he agonized like a woman in childbirth until Jesus Christ was formed in them (Galatians 4:19). The Greek word for formed (*morphothe*; NLT: "fully developed") means the essential form rather than the outward shape. The idea is of real Christlikeness—not external, formal compliance but true Christlikeness in thought, attitude, and motive.

   c. Answers will vary.

3. a. Peter preached the power (supernatural ability) of Jesus Christ and His second coming. While Peter could have emphasized a number of other important doctrines (devotion, worship, grace, death to self,

stewardship, missions, loving others, etc.), he preached Christ and the second coming. True God-honoring preaching exalts the person and power of Jesus Christ and His soon return.

b. 1. Man-made religious traditions (Mark 7:8–13). 2. Man-made philosophies that contradict God's Word (Colossians 2:8). 3. Unprovable religious myths and genealogies (e.g., "Da Vinci Code," "Gospel of Thomas"). 4. The Old Testament Law of Moses but misinterpreting it and teaching it incorrectly to others (1 Timothy 1:7–9). 5. Feel-good messages that don't deal with the whole truth of God's Word, including the more challenging portions of God's Word (2 Timothy 4:3–4).

4. Peter said the transfiguration confirmed the message of the Old Testament prophets (the prophetic word). In other words, both the Old Testament prophets and what Jesus spoke conveyed the same message.

5. a. Peter exhorted his readers to pay close attention to the Word since it is like a light shining in a dark place.

b. It is likely a reference to the return of Jesus Christ. This will happen at the end of the church age and before the great tribulation described in the book of Revelation.

c. He said believers would not escape if they neglected the Word of God (Hebrews 2:1–3). This doesn't mean they would perish, but believers are not immune from God's temporal judgment as a result of sin stemming from their neglect of God's Word.

6. # 4. In 1 Peter 1:17–18, Peter stated that what he heard on the Mount of Transfiguration confirmed the truthfulness of the Old Testament prophets' message (the prophetic word). Since most of the prophets did not know each other (they were separated by time and place), and Christ came many years later, the only way this could have happened (i.e., total consistency of message) was through divine inspiration. The prophets didn't just think these ideas up in their minds (**any private interpretation**; **never came by the will of man**; they were guided by the Holy Spirit who directed them to say and write exactly what God desired).

7. a. #3.

b. The Bible claims to be divinely inspired by God Himself so that every word is exactly what He wanted to communicate to man.

c. John 10:35 means that there is no error in the Scriptures. They cannot be divided into the inerrant words of God and the errant words of man. The theory that the Bible is a compilation of God's Word and man's writings is inaccurate.

8. In 2 Timothy 3:16 the Bible identifies the fourfold ministry of God's Word. The Bible teaches us how to live (that's **doctrine**), where we went wrong (that's **reproof**), how to get back on the right path (that's **correction**), and how to stay on the right path (that's **instruction in righteousness**). The Scriptures' purpose is realized when the child of God is "perfect, thoroughly furnished unto all good works" (v. 17 KJV).

Lesson 3: False Teachers

1. a. God used the false prophets to test the Israelites to see whether they would love the Lord with all their heart and with all their soul (Deuteronomy 13:4).
   b. God gave His people a simple, foolproof plan. One hundred percent of what a prophet prophesied had to come to pass, or else the person was exposed as a false prophet. If someone presumed to speak for God and the thing they "prophesied" did not come to pass, the people would know that the person was a false prophet. Note: If this simple plan was applied to so-called "prophets of God" today, a great number of the people who claim to speak for God would be exposed as false prophets.
   c. The death penalty.

2. a. The words that the older prophet spoke contradicted what God has previously told him (v. 9). In a previous situation, the prophet told the king that he was commanded by God not to eat any food and to return to his home by another route. Later when a "man of God" invited him to eat at his home, he became confused about what to do. The younger prophet should have declined the second offer and obeyed God.
   b. Stick tenaciously to the Word of God. Don't become confused about what some person says or about what a well-known religious leader says. Study your Bible. Read it carefully, study it in context, and believe what it teaches. The late American president Dwight Eisenhower said, "It is impossible to enslave a Bible-reading people."

3. Ravenous wolves (Matthew 7:15). Savage wolves (Acts 20:29–30).

4. a. Religious infidels (religious nonbelievers). They profess to know God and may have made a confession of faith (2 Peter 2:20–21), but the Bible says they are reserved for the day of judgment (2 Peter 3:9) and darkness forever (2 Peter 3:17). Moreover, references to them as dogs and pigs (v. 22)—a term that refers to those outside the family of God—indicate they are not part of the true family of God.

   b. The Greek word (*agorazo*) used for "bought" means Christ paid for their redemption even though they were not saved (see also 2 John 2:2). Christ's death on the cross was sufficient, but it was not efficient in the sense that they were never called unto salvation through faith.

5. 1. They often introduce heresies by asking questions to test the receptivity of their listeners.

   2. They quote others who espouse their heretical views to test the receptivity of their listeners.

   3. They cast doubt on the authority of God's Word (Genesis 3:1).

   4. They establish a culture of teaching selective portions of God's Word, and the people become weak in their faith (2 Timothy 4:3–4).

   5. Other answers could apply.

6. a. 1. Deceptive (vs. 1, 3). 2. Covetous (vs. 3, 14). 3. Carnal (v. 10). 4. Prideful and arrogant (v. 10). 5. Presumptuous (v. 10). 6. Self-willed (v. 10). 7. Lustful (v. 14). 8. Predatory (v. 14). 9. Willfully disobedient to God (v. 15).

   b. They often prey on emotionally unstable people (v. 14) and speak eloquently (**swelling words**; v. 18) but with little content (**words of emptiness**; v. 18). They appeal to the fleshly nature of their audience (**allure through the lusts of the flesh**; v. 18). Note: Many of the "Prosperity Gospel" preachers are an example of this.

   c. Their methods are covert (v. 1), deceptive (v. 3), bold and territorial (v. 12), predatory (v. 14), persuasive (v. 18), pompous (v. 18).

   d. So many believers will be deceived that the way of truth (the Christian faith) will be maligned.

7. a. 1. God's judgment is impartial. He will judge even the angels who abode with Him (2 Peter 2:4).

2. God's judgment is extensive. He will judge all those who rebel against His will (2 Peter 2:5).

3. God's judgment is severe. He absolutely destroyed the cities of Sodom and Gomorrah (2 Peter 2:6).

b. Every person needs to be sure that he is saved and walking with God. Believers need to all warn those who are not saved and those who are not living according to God's will.

8. a. The false teachers' minds were preoccupied with the thought of illicit sexual relations. They could hardly look at a woman without thinking of having sex with her. Their eyes were full of adulterous thoughts.

b. Answers will vary.

Lesson 4: The Day of the Lord

1. Peter wanted to stir his readers to greater spiritual devotion to God by reminding them of the words (writings) of the Old Testament prophets and the words of the apostles (1 Peter 3:1–2).

2. a. 1. Satan steals the truths of God's Word (Luke 8:12). Generally, this happens to those who are unsaved and believers who don't place great value on the Word.

   2. Persecution and testing cause others to fall away from the truth (Luke 8:13). These people fall away from the truth and forfeit God's peace.

   3. Life's worries and the pursuit of riches and pleasures prevent other believers from reaching spiritual maturity (Luke 8:14).

b. Answers will vary.

c. Answers will vary.

3. 1. The Old Testament (**whatever things were written before**) was written to teach us (Romans 15:4). Specifically, the believer learns patience and endurance (Gk. *hupomone*, steadfastness in the face of adversities) as he sees God deliver His people if they trust completely in Him (Romans 15:4).

   2. The Old Testament gives Christians hope as they see God's love and care for His people (Romans 15:4).

   3. The Old Testament also serves to warn or admonish Christians (1

Corinthians 10:11). The believer can be admonished to take a certain path in life or to avoid a specific decision based upon a similar situation that he can read about in the Scriptures.

4. The Old Testament instructs believers what is right (**doctrine**), where they went wrong (**reproof**), how to get right (**correction**), and how to stay right (**instruction in righteousness**) (2 Timothy 3:16–17).
Note: These same principles apply to the New Testament because all Scripture (not just the Old Testament) is inspired by God.

4. a. Their argument was since Jesus Christ has not returned yet, He will never return (2 Peter 3:4). This is the argument of rational constancy. Interestingly, it is the same argument that evolutionists use for the theory of an old earth. They believe that the earth must be billions of years old since the fossil record, the development of man, and the presence of microorganisms require it. Their theory is based upon the "constancy of life" principle that rejects the Genesis flood and its effects.

b. The scoffers deliberately reject the idea of Christ's return. They know that Christ's return means their judgment, and they choose to intentionally ignore this reality. "Deliberately ignore." "Willfully ignorant." Other answers could apply.

c. God's judgment on the earth has already happened once in the past. Scoffers should not ignore the fact that it will happen again (2 Peter 3:5). The Genesis flood was not simply a natural disaster. It was God's divine judgment on the world, and it came suddenly. Peter said that God's judgment would come a second time, not in the form of a worldwide flood but in the form of an intense heat.

5. a. It is not proper hermeneutics (the principles of interpretation). You shouldn't take a portion of a verse to support an interpretation when the verse also presents the opposite.

b. God doesn't always measure time in the same way man does.

c. God is not willing for any to perish (a reference to eternal judgment) but for all to come to repentance. The truth is that not all men will be saved. Universalism or universal salvation is not taught in the Bible. Everyone will know that God waited patiently for all men to come to the knowledge of the truth.

6. a. God will destroy the world because of the wickedness in it (2 Peter 3:7). The heavens—the atmospheric heaven (not the abode of God)—will pass away with a great noise, and the world and its works will be burned up (2 Peter 3:10).

    b. Believers should live godly lives (2 Peter 3:11) and seek to reach the lost before the coming judgment (2 Peter 3:12).

7. 1. There will be a new heavens and earth, and only righteousness will dwell on the new earth (2 Peter 3:13). 2. There will be no more sea (Revelation 21:1). 3. A new city called the New Jerusalem, the tabernacle of God, will be located there (Revelation 21:2–3). 4. There will be no sorrow, crying, or death (Revelation 21:4). 5. The New Jerusalem will be surrounded by a great, high wall with three gates in each side (Revelation 21:10, 13), each gate bearing the name of one of the twelve tribes of Israel (Revelation 21:12). 6. There will be no night in the New Jerusalem, as God and Jesus will be the light for the city (Revelation 21:22–23). 7. The nations and the kings of the earth will bring glory and honor to God (Revelation 21:24).

8. a. Peter warns his readers to be careful not to fall away from the Lord by believing the lies of the wicked.

    b. To grow in grace and in the knowledge of their Lord and Savior, Jesus Christ.

Lesson 5: Contend for the Faith

1. 1. They are **called** by God. In man's natural (unsaved condition) state, he is spiritually dead (Ephesians 2:1–3) and is completely blind to God's true nature and worth (2 Corinthians 4:4). He is incapable of responding to God, not just unwilling to (1 Corinthians 2:14). The unregenerate man hides from God so his evil deeds are not exposed (John 3:19–20). God draws man to Himself through the convicting power of the Holy Spirit (John 16:8–11), and those who are effectively called are also redeemed. God's call does not eliminate man's need for repentance and in faith in Christ (Acts 16:30–31).

    2. They are (positionally) **sanctified** by God.

    3. They are **preserved** (or secure) in Jesus Christ.

2. a. 1. Secular education, including secular colleges and universities where the Christian faith is often attacked or marginalized.

2. The portion of the entertainment industry (movies, TV, videos, books, gaming, etc.) that presents sinful conduct (murder, theft, lying, drug use, immorality, etc.) without accurately presenting the personal consequences and sin's harmful impact on others.

b. 1. Pray. Support Christian education at all levels, and promote truth in public education. Encourage Christian educators to stand up for the truth, and stand with them in their struggle. Encourage Christians attending public schools to be active in their faith and join good Bible-believing churches.

2. Don't support the entertainment industry with your dollars whenever Christian values are undermined. Other answers could apply.

3. Since the Bible teaches that the Christian faith was once for all delivered to the saints (i.e., believers), there is no continuing revelation through self-proclaimed prophets. God's revelation to man has been completed.

4. a. The doctrine of grace and the doctrine of Christ (Christology).

b. 1. The imposters entered Christian assemblies secretly (Jude 4).

2. The imposters took the doctrine of grace and twisted it to say something else (Jude 4).

3. They used flowery speech and flattered people and appealed to the fleshly appetite of man (Jude 16).

c. Church leaders and entire congregations should implement a scriptural vetting process that includes examining all potential teachers and leaders on the basis of doctrinal soundness and godly character. Candidates for a pastoral office should meet the biblical requirements for spiritual leaders (1 Timothy 3:1-12) and should be totally committed to the truth.

5. a. Believers are not supposed to use their liberty or freedom in Christ to satisfy their own fleshly desires.

b. 1. Christians are not to let the expression of their freedom in Christ become a stumbling block to weak believers (1 Corinthians 8:9).

2. Paul said he would never eat meat (or do anything) again if it caused another Christian to stumble in his relationship with Christ (1 Corinthians 8:13).

3. Paul said he would adapt as far as he could so others would be saved (1 Corinthians 9:19–22).

6. a. Sodom and Gomorrah and the other cities were judged because of their sexual immorality, including homosexual behavior (**strange flesh**; Jude 7; NIV: "perversion").
   b. These cities are presented as an example of God's judgment on those who violate His standard of sexual conduct.

7. The believer should have a healthy respect for the reality and power of the demonic world. He should realize that, in his flesh, he isn't able to overcome the spiritual forces of evil but is able to overcome every spiritual attack if he trusts completely in God and puts on the whole armor of God (Ephesians 6:10–18). The believer must also realize God is abiding within him (through the Holy Spirit's abiding presence), and He is greater than any demonic spirit in this world (1 John 4:2–4).

8. They were dreamers (Jude 8). They defiled or polluted their own bodies with sin (Jude 8). They rejected authority, becoming a law unto themselves (Jude 8). The use of the Greek word (*kurioteta*: lordship) likely means they openly rejected the authority of Jesus Christ over their lives. They slandered celestial beings (Jude 8). It appears they rejected all authority (earthly and heavenly, good and evil) because they were a law unto themselves (Jude 8, 10). They functioned solely from the perspective of perceived fleshly gratification (Jude 10). In this way, they acted like animals (Jude 10).

Lesson 6: Faultless in His Presence

1. a. 1. They have gone the way of Cain. 2. They have run greedily in the error of Balaam. 3. They have perished in the rebellion of Korah.
   b. Cain worshipped God according to his own desires and terms— not those prescribed by the Lord (Genesis 4:5, 7). The biblical text implies that God had instructed both Cain and Abel regarding what He expected for an acceptable sacrifice. The spiritual imposters, like Cain, sought to establish their own form of approaching God in worship. Today, worshippers follow the "way of Cain" when they seek to worship God according to their own ideas—such as doing good

works, etc.—rather than believing in Jesus Christ alone for eternal life and walking in God's will.

    c.   Balaam was an Old Testament prophet who was a prototype of all greedy religious teachers. On one hand, Balaam seemed constrained to speak for God, but on the other hand he wanted to financially profit from the use of his position. In the same way, the spiritual imposters wanted to feast on the believers and were willing to say whatever would give them an advantage (Jude 16).

2.   Jude describes their judgment as having already taken place because of its certainty. Since God is omniscient (all-knowing), He knows the future, which includes the day of judgment that will come upon all who reject Him.

3.   1. Clouds without water (Jude 12). In the arid climate of the Middle East, the sight of clouds brings hope of rain and the possibility of temporary relief from the intense heat. Like clouds without water, the spiritual imposters brought temporary hope but produced no relief. 2. Autumn trees without fruit. Israel is a rich, fruit-producing land, and a fruit tree without fruit is worthless (Jude 12). The imposters were fruitless and spiritually dead. 3. Raging waves that produce only foam (Jude 13). In many places, raging waves crashing on the shore bring a harvest of edible crustaceans. The imposters were loud and bold like the raging sea, but they brought nothing of value. 4. Wandering or shooting stars (Jude 13). The stars provided direction and navigation for sailors, but a wandering or shooting star produced a sudden burst of light that was of no value. The imposters burst on the scene in a blaze of light (notoriety) but were gone quickly.

4.   Answers will vary.

5.   They are ungodly. They do ungodly deeds. They do their ungodly deeds in an ungodly way. Note: Jude's use of the triad (union or group of three) is a significant linguistic tool that is used repeatedly throughout the book (Jude 1, 2, 8, 11, 15, 19).

6.   They are grumblers (Jude 16), complainers (Jude 16), self-centered (Jude 16), big talkers (Jude 16), flatterers (Jude 16), sensual or lustful (Jude 19), divisive (Jude 19), unsaved (Jude 19), and devoid of the Spirit.

7. a. 1. The believers were to remember the words of the apostles (Jude 17). For believers today, that would be the entire New Testament. They were to remember that the apostles warned them about spiritual mockers (Jude 18) who live according to their own ways. 2. They were also able to build themselves up in the faith (Jude 20). 3. They were to pray in the Holy Spirit (Jude 20). This means to be alert and sensitive to the Holy Spirit's leading so they pray according to the will of God. 4. They were to keep themselves in the love of God (Jude 21). 5. They were to look to the return of Christ when His mercy will be given to all those who fully trusted in Him (Jude 21).

    b. To keep yourself in the love of God means to stay in close fellowship with God so that the trials, temptations, disappointments with others, and additional setbacks and obstacles don't discourage you to the point of falling away from the Lord.

    c. Have compassion on them and rescue them (Jude 22).

    d. Believers must learn to hate sin and the effect it has on those who fall deeply into its grasp. The Christian should fear sin and its power to corrupt and defile all those made in the image of God. Jude's statement of hating even the garment defiled by sin presents a graphic image of the totality of sin's effects—namely that even the garments are defiled. What a picture of sin's impact and the attitude that God's people should have toward all sin.

8. He is God and Savior, all-wise, worthy of glory, majesty, dominion and power.

9. God alone is truly wise. For this reason, He alone deserved glory and majesty, dominion and power. He is the only one worthy of praise and adoration.

10. Answers will vary.

FINAL EXAM

Every person will eventually stand before God in judgment—the final exam. The Bible says, ***And it is appointed for men to die once, but after this the judgment*** (Hebrews 9:27).

May I ask you a question? *If you died today, do you know for certain you would go to heaven?* I did not ask if you're religious or a church member, nor did I ask if you've had some encounter with God—a meaningful spiritual experience. I didn't even ask if you believe in God or angels or if you're trying to live a good life. The question I *am* asking is this: *If you died today, do you know for certain you would go to heaven?*

When you die, you will stand alone before God in judgment. You'll either be saved for all eternity, or you will be separated from God for all eternity in what the Bible calls the lake of fire (Romans 14:12; Revelation 20:11–15). Tragically, many religious people who believe in God are not going to be accepted by Him when they die.

> ***Many will say to Me in that day, "Lord, Lord, have we not prophesied in Your name, cast out demons in Your name, and done many wonders in Your name?" And then I will declare to them, "I never knew you; depart from Me, you who practice lawlessness!"*** (Matthew 7:22–23)

God loves you and wants you to go to heaven (John 3:16; 2 Peter 3:9). If you are not sure where you'll spend eternity, you are not prepared to meet God. God wants you to know for certain that you will go to heaven.

> ***Behold, now is the accepted time; behold, now is the day of salvation.*** (2 Corinthians 6:2)

The words ***behold*** and ***now*** are repeated because God wants you to know that you can be saved today. You do not need to hear those terrible words, ***Depart from Me ....*** Isn't that great news?

Jesus himself said, ***You must be born again*** (John 3:7). These aren't the words of a pastor, a church, or a particular denomination. They're the words of Jesus Christ himself. You *must* be born again (saved from eternal damnation) before you die; otherwise, it will be too late when you die! You can know for certain today that God will accept you into heaven when you die.

*These things I have written to you who believe in the name of the Son of God, that you may **know** that you have eternal life.*

(1 John 5:13)

The phrase **you may know** means that you can know for certain before you die that you will go to heaven. To be born again, you must understand and accept four essential spiritual truths. These truths are right from the Bible, so you know you can trust them—they are not man-made religious traditions. Now, let's consider these four essential spiritual truths.

Essential Spiritual Truth

#1

The Bible teaches that you are a sinner and separated from God.

No one is righteous in God's eyes. To be righteous means to be totally without sin, not even a single act.

There is none righteous, no, not one;
There is none who understands;
There is none who seeks after God.
They have all turned aside;
They have together become unprofitable;
There is none who does good, no, not one.
(Romans 3:10–12)

...for all have sinned and fall short of the glory of God.
(Romans 3:23)

Look at the words God uses to show that all men are sinners—**none, not one, all turned aside, not one**. God is making a point: all of us are sinners. No one is good (perfectly without sin) in His sight. The reason is sin.

Have you ever lied, lusted, hated someone, stolen anything, or taken God's name in vain, even once? These are all sins.

Are you willing to admit to God that you are a sinner? If so, then tell Him right now you have sinned. You can say the words in your heart or aloud—it doesn't matter which—but be honest with God. Now check the box if you have just admitted you are a sinner.

☐   God, I admit I am a sinner in Your eyes.

Now, let's look at the second essential spiritual truth.

Essential Spiritual Truth

#2

The Bible teaches that you cannot save yourself or earn your way to heaven.

Man's sin is a very serious problem in the eyes of God. Your sin separates you from God, both now and for all eternity—unless you are born again.

For the wages of sin is death.
(Romans 6:23)

And you He made alive, who were dead in trespasses and sins.
(Ephesians 2:1)

Wages are a payment a person earns by what he or she has done. Your sin has earned you the wages of death, which means separation from God. If you die never having been born again, you will be separated from God after death.

You cannot save yourself or purchase your entrance into heaven. The Bible says that man is **not redeemed with corruptible things, like silver or gold** (1 Peter 1:18). If you owned all the money in the world, you still could not buy your entrance into heaven. Neither can you buy your way into heaven with good works.

For by grace you have been saved through faith, and that not of yourselves; it is the gift of God, not of works, lest anyone should boast. (Ephesians 2:8–9)

The Bible says salvation is **not of yourselves**. It is **not of works, lest anyone should boast**. Salvation from eternal judgment cannot be earned by doing good works; it is a gift of God. There is nothing you can do to purchase your way into heaven because you are already unrighteous in God's eyes.

If you understand you cannot save yourself, then tell God right now that you are a sinner, separated from Him, and you cannot save yourself. Check the box below if you have just done that.

☐ God, I admit that I am separated from You because of my sin. I realize that I cannot save myself.

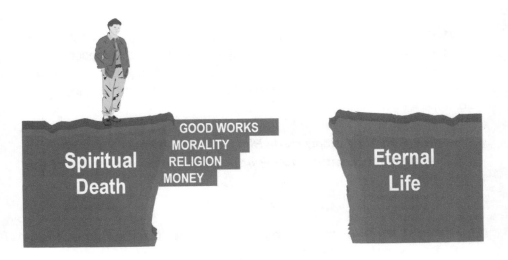

Now, let's look at the third essential spiritual truth.

Essential Spiritual Truth

#3

The Bible teaches that Jesus Christ died on the cross to pay the complete penalty for your sin and to purchase a place in heaven for you.

Jesus Christ, the sinless Son of God, lived a perfect life, died on the cross, and rose from the dead to pay the penalty for your sin and purchase a place in heaven for you. He died on the cross on your behalf, in your place, as your substitute, so you do not have to go to hell. Jesus Christ is the only acceptable substitute for your sin.

For He [God, the Father] made Him [Jesus] who knew [committed] no sin to be sin for us, that we might become the righteousness of God in Him.
(2 Corinthians 5:21)

I [Jesus] am the way, the truth, and the life. No one comes to the Father except through Me.
(John 14:6)

Nor is there salvation in any other, for there is no other name under heaven given among men by which we must be saved.
(Acts 4:12)

Jesus Christ is your only hope and means of salvation. Because you are a sinner, you cannot pay for your sins, but Jesus paid the penalty for your sins by dying on the cross in your place. Friend, there is salvation in no one else—not angels, not some religious leader, not even your religious good works. No religious act such as baptism, confirmation, or joining a church can save you. There is no other way, no other name that can save you. Only Jesus Christ can save you. You must be saved by accepting Jesus Christ's substitutionary sacrifice for your sins, or you will be lost forever.

Do you see clearly that Jesus Christ is the only way to God in heaven? If you understand this truth, tell God that you understand, and check the box below.

❏ God, I understand that Jesus Christ died to pay the penalty for my sin. I understand that His death on the cross was the only acceptable sacrifice for my sin.

Spiritual Death

Eternal Life

Essential Spiritual Truth

#4

By faith, you must trust in Jesus Christ alone for eternal life and call upon Him to be your Savior and Lord.

Many religious people admit they have sinned. They believe Jesus Christ died for the sins of the world, but they are not saved. Why? Thousands of moral, religious people have never completely placed their faith in Jesus Christ *alone* for eternal life. They think they must believe in Jesus Christ as a real person and do good works to earn their way to heaven. They are not trusting Jesus Christ alone. To be saved, you must trust in Jesus Christ *alone* for eternal life. Look what the Bible teaches about trusting Jesus Christ alone for salvation.

Believe on the Lord Jesus Christ, and you will be saved.
(Acts 16:31)

...that if you confess with your mouth the Lord Jesus and believe in your heart that God has raised Him from the dead, you will be saved. For with the heart one believes unto righteousness, and with the mouth confession is made unto salvation.... For there is no distinction between Jew and Greek, for the same Lord over all is rich to all who call upon Him. For "whoever calls on the name of the Lord shall be saved.
(Romans 10:9–10, 12–13)

Do you see what God is saying? To be saved or born again, you must trust Jesus Christ *alone* for eternal life. Jesus Christ paid for your complete salvation. Jesus said, **It is finished!** (John 19:30). Jesus paid for your salvation completely when He shed His blood on the cross for your sin.

If you believe that God resurrected Jesus Christ (proving God's acceptance of Jesus as a worthy sacrifice for man's sin) and you are willing to confess Jesus Christ as your Savior and Lord (master of your life), you will be saved.

Friend, right now God is offering you the greatest gift in the world. God wants to give you the *gift* of eternal life, the *gift* of His complete forgiveness for all your sins, and the *gift* of His unconditional acceptance into heaven when you die. Will you accept His free gift now, right where you are?

Are you unsure how to receive the gift of eternal life? Let me help you. Do you remember that I said you needed to understand and accept four essential spiritual truths? First, you admitted you are a sinner. Second, you admitted you were separated from God because of your sin and you could not save yourself. Third, you realized that Jesus Christ is the only way to heaven—no other name can save you.

Now, you must trust that Jesus Christ died once and for all to save your lost soul. Just take God at His word—He will not lie to you! This is the kind of simple faith you need to be saved. If you would like to be saved right now, right where you are, offer this prayer of simple faith to God. Remember, the words must come from your heart.

God, I am a sinner and deserve to go to hell. Thank You, Jesus, for dying on the cross for me and for purchasing a place in heaven for me. I believe You are the Son of God and You are able to save me right now. Please forgive me for my sin and take me to heaven when I die. I invite You into my life as Savior and Lord, and I trust You alone for eternal life. Thank You for giving me the gift of eternal life. Amen.

If, in the best way you know how, you trusted Jesus Christ alone to save you, then God just saved you. He said in His Holy Word, ***But as many as received Him, to them He gave the right to become the children of God*** (John 1:12). It's that simple. God just gave you the gift of eternal life by faith. You have just been born again, according to the Bible.

You will not come into eternal judgment, and you will not perish in the lake of fire—you are saved forever! Read this verse carefully and let it sink into your heart.

> *Most assuredly, I say to you, he who hears My word and believes in Him who sent Me has everlasting life, and shall not come into judgment, but has passed from death into life.*
> (John 5:24)

Now, let me ask you a few more questions.

According to God's holy Word (John 5:24), not your feelings, what kind of life did God just give you? _____

What two words did God say at the beginning of the verse to assure you that He is not lying to you? _____ _____

Are you going to come into eternal judgment? ☐ YES ☐ NO

Have you passed from spiritual death into life? ☐ YES ☐ NO

Friend, you've just been born again. You just became a child of God.

To help you grow in your new Christian life, we would like to send you some Bible study materials. To receive these helpful materials free of charge, e-mail your request to **info@LamplightersUSA.org.**

Appendix

Level 1 (Basic Training)
Student Workbook

To begin, familiarize yourself with the Lamplighters' *Leadership Training and Development Process* (see graphic on page 72). Notice there are two circles: a smaller, inner circle and a larger, outer circle. The inner circle shows the sequence of weekly meetings beginning with an Open House, followed by an 8–14 week study, and concluding with a clear presentation of the gospel (Final Exam). The outer circle shows the sequence of the Intentional Discipleship training process (Leading Studies, Training Leaders, Multiplying Groups). As participants are transformed by God's Word, they're invited into a discipleship training process that equips them in every aspect of the intentional disciple-making ministry.

The Level 1 training (Basic Training) is *free*, and the training focuses on two key aspects of the training: 1) how to prepare a life-changing Bible study (ST-A-R-T) and 2) how to lead a life-changing Bible study (10 commandments). The training takes approximately 60 minutes to complete, and you complete it as an individual or collectively as a small group (preferred method) by inserting an extra week between the Final Exam and the Open House.

To begin your training, go to www.LamplightersUSA.org to register yourself or your group. A Lamplighters' Certified Trainer will guide you through the entire Level 1 training process. After you have completed the training, you can review as many times as you like.

When you have completed the Level 1 training, please consider completing the Level 2 (Advanced) training. Level 2 training will equip you to reach more people for Christ by learning how to train new leaders and by showing you how to multiply groups. You can register for additional training at www.LamplightersUSA.org.

Intentional Discipleship
Training & Development Process

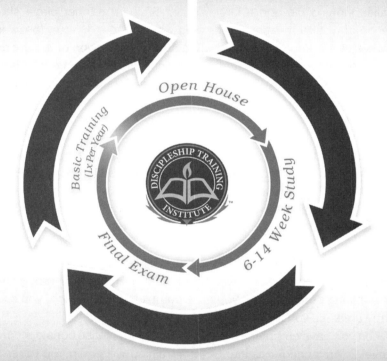

3. Multiplying Groups

*The "5 Steps" for Starting
New Groups
The Audio Training Library (ATL)
The Importance of the Open House*

1. Leading Studies

*ST-A-R-T
10 Commandments
Solving All Group Problems*

2. Training Leaders

*Four-fold ministry of a leader
The Three Diagnostic Questions*

*The 2P's for recruiting new leaders
The three stages of leadership training*

How to Prepare a Life-Changing Bible Study
ST-A-R-T

Step 1: _____ and _____.

    Pray specifically for the group members and yourself as you study God's Word. Ask God (_____) to give each group member a rich time of personal Bible study, and thank (_____) God for giving you a desire to invest in the spiritual advancement of each other.

Step 2: _____ the _____.

    Answer the questions in the weekly lessons without looking at the _____ _____.

Step 3: _____and _____.

    Review the Leader's Guide, and _____ every truth you missed when you originally did your lesson. Record the answers you missed with a _____ _____ so you'll know what you missed.

Step 4: _____ _____.

    Calculate the specific amount of time _____ _____ to spend on each question and write the start time next to each one in the _____ using a _____.

How to Lead a Life-Changing Bible Study

10 COMMANDMENTS

1	2	3
4	5	6
7	8	9
	10	

Lamplighters' 10 Commandments are proven small group leadership principles that have been used successfully to train hundreds of believers to lead life-changing, intentional discipleship Bible studies.

Essential Principles for Leading Intentional Discipleship Bible Studies

1. The 1st Commandment: The _____ Rule.
   The Leader-Trainer should be in the room _____ minutes before the class begins.

2. The 2nd Commandment: The _____-_____ Rule.
   Train the group that it is okay to _____, but they should never be
   _____.

3. The 3rd Commandment: The _____ Rule.
   _____, _____, _____ ask for
   _____ to _____ the _____, _____, and _____
   the questions. The Leader-Trainer, however, should always _____ the
   questions to control the _____ of the study.

4. The 4th Commandment: The ____:____ Rule.
   _____ the Bible study on time and _____ the study on time
   _____ _____. No exceptions!

5. The 5th Commandment: The _____ Rule.
   Train the group participants to _____ on God's Word for answers
   to life's questions.

1	2	3
4 **59:59**	5	6
7	8	9
	10	

6. The 6th Commandment: The _____ Rule.
   Deliberately and progressively _____ _____ participants into the group discussion over a period of time.

7. The 7th Commandment: The _____ _____ Rule.
   _____ the participants to get _____ the answers to the questions, not just _____ or _____ ones.

8. The 8th Commandment: The _____ Rule.
   _____ the group discussion so you _____ the lesson _____ _____ and give each question _____ _____.

9. The 9th Commandment: The _____-_____ Rule.
   Don't let the group members talk about _____ _____, _____ _____, or _____ _____.

10. The 10th Commandment: The _____ Rule.
   _____ God to change lives, including _____.

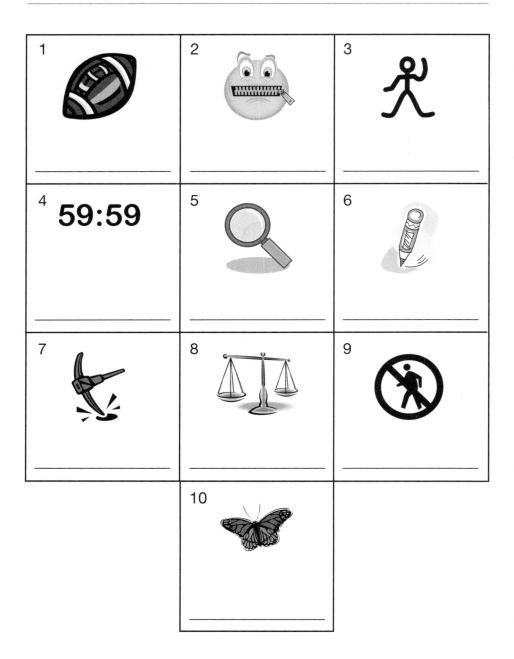

Choose your next study from any of the following titles

- John 1-11
- John 12-21
- Acts 1-12
- Acts 13-28
- Romans 1-8
- Romans 9-16
- Galatians
- Ephesians
- Philippians

- Colossians
- 1 & 2 Thessalonians
- 1 Timothy
- 2 Timothy
- Titus/Philemon
- Hebrews
- James
- 1 Peter
- 2 Peter/Jude

Additional Bible studies and sample lessons
are available online.

For audio introductions on all Bible studies,
visit us online at www.Lamplightersusa.org.

Looking to begin a new group?
The Lamplighters Starter Kit includes:

- 8 James Bible Study Guides
  (students purchase their own books)
- 25 Welcome Booklets
- 25 Table Tents
- 25 Bible Book Locator Bookmarks
- 50 Final Exam Tracts
- 50 Invitation Cards

For a current listing of live and online discipleship training
events, or to register for discipleship training, go to
www.LamplightersUSA.org/training.